SIMPLY STROLLING

Simply Strolling

Easy flat walks in North Wales,

*with no bogs, stiles, steep climbs,
or scrambles, and
always a place to stop for a break*

by Gill Meyer

ISBN: 978-1-84524-262-6

Cover design: Carreg Gwalch
Cover image and main images inside:

Published by Gwasg Carreg Gwalch,
12 Iard yr Orsaf, Llanrwst, Wales LL26 0EH
tel: 01492 642031
fax: 01492 641502
email: books@carreg-gwalch.com
website: www.carreg-gwalch.com

Contents

Acknowledgements

My sincere thanks go to my husband Bob, for his great support; and all the members of the Dyffryn Conwy Strollers Walking Group. They are a loyal source of inspiration and suggestions regarding where we might consider for a walk in the future, and they bear the challenges of our ever-changing beautiful Welsh weather with general good nature and a laugh. None of us will forget walking round part of Llyn Brenig in horizontal sleet!

My special thanks go to Roger and Angela Prince for a significant number of photographs, and to Keith Roobotham for his close-up image of the grey seals. I am also very grateful for the images of Tu Hwnt i'r Bont and Tŷ Hyll that Tim Maddox kindly provided.

Some of the Dyffryn Conwy Strollers Walking Group

I would like to offer a special note of appreciation to all the cafés, restaurants, pubs and hotels that are mentioned in this book. They have coped with us brilliantly!

Thank you to everyone.

Introduction

This book is for those of us who, for a variety of reasons do not choose to walk that far, clamber over stiles, boggy or very uneven ground, up mountains, or long steep hills. However, we believe that it is still possible to thoroughly enjoy the Welsh landscape from the comfort of sea level, or above, if a car, bus or train can get us to the start of the walk! The distances are between 2 and almost 5 miles (3-8 kilometres). Many can be extended significantly, as they might be sections of longer routes.

You will discover warm welcomes in little cafés, or even hotels, where you can stop for a coffee or lunch, to break the walk, or to relax in at the end.

The strolls are as varied as the places you will stop at. We offer you town strolls, country and riverside or lakeside ambles, and even a flat stroll at 1200 feet. Do enjoy discovering some hidden gems.

Where a stroll is suitable for wheelchair users, or strollers, the logos below will be used. Please note that some of the strolls might be suitable for wheelchair users for just part of the way.

Some cafés or pubs will allow dogs inside, but in the main owners are asked to use the outside seating areas. Where dogs are welcomed by proprietors I use the doggy logo. Please note that this information is accurate at the time of printing, and may change because of new ownership. Please check with the proprietors if they still allow dogs inside, in case the policy has changed.

Happy strolling!

Gill Meyer

Area covered by strolls

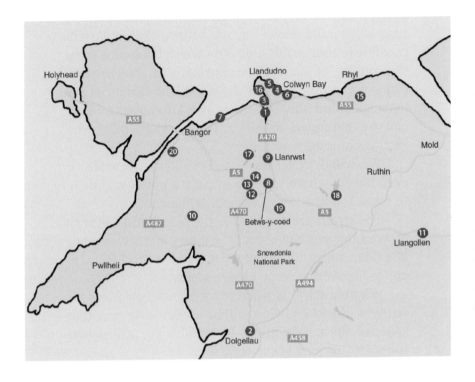

Many of the strolls are in, or close to the Conwy Valley, a particularly beautiful part of the country. The river Conwy rises near the tiny and charming village of Ysbyty Ifan, which is south of Betws-y-coed, off the A5, and it reaches the sea at Deganwy and West Shore, Llandudno.

Snowdonia National Park offers the stunning sight of the Snowdon Horseshoe and the surrounding impressive mountains. Further east, and south, the land is less mountainous, except for the Berwyn Mountains which are equally beautiful, lying south of Corwen. Areas of high moorland, and more rolling countryside are found especially as you travel south towards Dolgellau.

The regions of Betws-y-coed and Llanrwst have many abandoned mines, as this has been a mineral rich area since Roman times... Notably copper, lead, and silver. If you visit Cricieth beach and look at the fine shingle on the water's edge there, you will see the huge variety of different types and colours of stones.

Enjoy the wildlife here, and nature in general. Pack your waterproof each time you walk. There is a good reason for this part of the world being so green!

Stroll No 1

RSPB Nature Reserve going north alongside the Conwy estuary

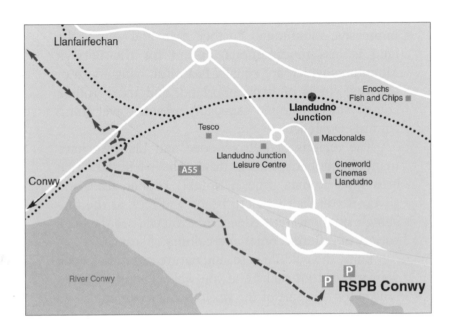

How to get there:

By Car: *Take Junction 18 off the A55, follow the brown signs for The Nature Reserve, come off the slip road and take the first turning on your left (if you have been travelling west). The road leading to The Nature Reserve leads down to the estuary where sometimes it is possible to park. This will be the starting point, where you will stroll towards the water and then turn right, where you will see the path alongside the estuary.*

If you cannot park here, follow the road round, into the Nature Reserve car park. There is no charge for parking here.

By Bus: *There is no bus service to the Nature Reserve.*

By Train: *There is no easy and safe route from Llandudno Junction station to the Nature Reserve.*

Distance: *3.2 miles (5.15 kilometres).*

Route of stroll:

On leaving the Bird reserve Car Park, take the estuary side path towards Deganwy. Pass over the sloped pedestrian footbridge over the railway. You might choose to go as far as the Deganwy Quay Hotel (quay hotel.co.uk), and call there for a coffee on the terrace, before walking back. This will be 1.6 miles each way (2.5 kilometres).

Comments:

This is a wide flat path which is fine even after rain, with good views of Conwy, the castle, and hills around. The bird life is fascinating, especially when the tide is low. At the end of the walk pop into the RSPB Bird Reserve (rspb.org.uk) if you did not pause at the Deganwy Quay Hotel, and have a little of what you

Coastal Path near RSPB

The Cob leading to Conwy

The Conwy Estuary

fancy! There are sometimes telescopes/binoculars in the café which can be used free of charge to watch the birds while you are there.

Although this stroll is absolutely flat, the very beginning approx. (10-15 yds.) is rather rough ground and sloped down towards the water. It might be too uneven for a wheelchair, but pushchairs/buggies can be pushed with care over this initial stretch. The pedestrian footbridge over the railway is sloped, but there are no steps.

The path does go beyond Deganwy, to West Shore Llandudno, but there is often quite considerable sand build on it which makes walking hard going on the legs and ankles!

Simply of Interest:

The river Conwy is over 27 miles long, and rises on the Migneint moor. It is fed by a number of tributaries, namely the rivers Machno and Lledr, and at Betws-y-coed it is joined by the river Llugwy. Further along, Afon Crafnant, and Afon Porth Llwyd and Afon Ddu also join it. During the Spring tides it is tidal as far as Tan Lan which is north of Llanrwst. As the river is so long with such a large catchment area, the valley does experience flooding. Consequently such flood plains do support quite rich ecosystems.

There is an ancient story about the river Conwy Afanc, a huge legendary Welsh water monster that was deemed to be responsible for terrible floods, so Afanc had to be enticed to a new home in Llyn Ffynnon Las, under the shadow of Snowdon...!

The RSPB Conwy was created after the building of the Conwy tunnel. There are a number of nature trails and hides with views over the water. The visiting birds change throughout the year with some coming from Africa in spring and summer, and others from the Arctic and Russia in winter. This is a lovely place to stroll round and to watch the birds and wildlife secretly from the hides!

Stroll No 2

The Mawddach Estuary

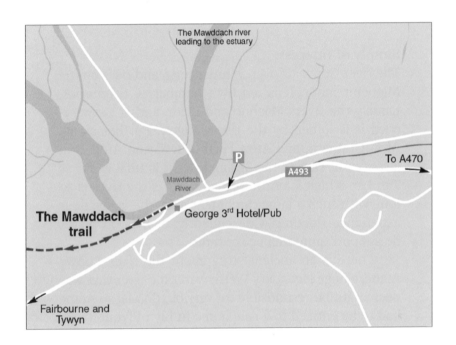

How to get there:

By Car: *Take the A470 south from Llanrwst, remaining on this road almost all the way, passing by Betws-y-coed, and through Blaenau Ffestiniog, and at Ffestiniog, you will be taking a sharp hairpin bend to the left going uphill... (be careful NOT to go straight ahead at this point, when the road becomes the B4391 which you do not want). You will later pass by Trawsfynnydd de commissioned power station, and the lake, which will be on your right. Coed y Brenin is a few miles ahead...*

Stay on the A470, until you turn right onto the A493 to Tywyn. After approx. a mile or so you will see a sign for the Penmaenuchaf Hotel. Continue a short distance and soon, you will see a small brown sign of a bed, on your left indicating a hotel. Turn right here. This is the George III Pub. There are two car parks. You will see the first immediately, the second is reached by driving in front of the pub, and you will find it on the left beyond the pub... The walk starts from this second car park, by following the trail off to the left.

By Bus/Train: *There is no direct bus or train service to Penmaenpool.*

Distance: *Flexible. 3 miles (4.8 kilometres). A there and back stroll, in this case. However, the Mawddach trail is actually 9.5 miles (15 km) long, extending from Dolgellau to Barmouth, so this route suits everyone!*

Route of stroll:

Pass in front of the pub and continue down the track. Follow the trail for as long as you wish, before turning back. (We often turn back after strolling for about 30-40 mins.) Enjoy a snack at the pub on your return.

Comments:

The drive down the A470 is beautiful, and has a wild rolling nature about it. The Mawddach trail is

The George III Hotel

The wooden toll bridge

The Mawddach Trail

absolutely flat, being an old railway embankment. There is the beauty of the Mawddach Estuary, its birdlife, wonderful wild flowers, and the cattle with their young might be a charming bonus.

You can pre order your lunch before setting off, to avoid a long wait. This pub is very popular and does get busy. (Website: georgethethird.co.uk). This is a dog friendly pub, but please check as policies and owners do change.

The trail is ideal for wheelchair users and pushchairs. It is wide and flat; since it used to be the railway route between Barmouth and Dolgellau.

Should you wish to stroll over the charming wooden toll bridge nearby, there is a charge of 20p for pedestrians, and 70p for cars.

Simply of Interest:

Penmaenpool is described as a hamlet, found on the south side of the Mawddach estuary. The George III pub/hotel dates back to 1650, It served the busy boat building industry at the time. It was originally two buildings, a ship chandler, and a pub. The wooden toll bridge was built in 1879 to replace a ferry service.

In 1966 there was a tragedy when a pleasure ferry hit the toll bridge, and 39 people lost their lives. The then proprietor and his chef helped to save many lives that day.

The Toll Bridge was built in 1879 to replace a ferry service.

There is an RSPB reserve in The Mawddach Valley, at Coed Garth Gell, which might be reached by going over the toll bridge and turning left onto the A496 and looking out for signposts thereafter. (see RSPB website: rspb.org.uk)

There used to be a railway station at Penmaenpool, but it closed in 1965. The original signal box has been used by the RSPB.

Stroll No 3

Llandudno Junction to Conwy Marina via Conwy quayside

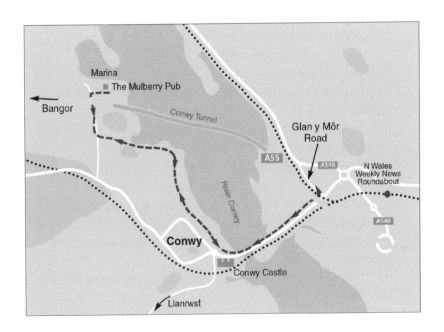

How to get there:

By Car: *Take the A470 to Llandudno Junction. At The North Wales Weekly News Roundabout, take the turning for A546 Deganwy and Llandudno, but do not go too fast, as you will need to take the first turning left which is Glan y Môr Rd. It leads to behind the Weekly News Building. Continue ahead until you are almost under the flyover. The old Arriva building is on your left. This is a good place to park (free).*

By Bus: *Buses go from Llandudno coach park to Conwy, stopping at the flyover (stop "W"). Cross the road to join the pavement and lower footpath along the cob towards Conwy.*

By Train: *Come out of Llandudno Junction station, turn left, walk along Conway Rd, which runs into Ferndale Rd, and takes you to the large North Wales Weekly News roundabout. With caution, cross the junction on your left and make for Conway Rd which leads directly to Conwy. You will need to be on the right hand side pavement as you face Conwy, this will lead you down to a lower footpath along the cob that leads into the town.*

Distance: *Approx. 4 miles (6.4 kilometres) i.e. 2 miles each way.*

Route of stroll:

Take the flight of 36 steps up to the road, or use the pedestrian slope opposite for easier/disabled access. Stroll over the cob to Conwy, along the quayside, and through the archway in the wall at the end. Continue up the road for a few yards (it goes uphill at this point), then bear right and slightly downhill onto the estuary side path. Follow this until you come out on a main road, turn right and follow the pavement/road as it goes over the A55. When you reach a junction, bear right and you will see that you are at The Mulberry pub/restaurant. Enjoy a break here. Return the same way as you came.

Comments:
The Mulberry Pub Conwy, (see Robinsons website: robinsonsbrewery.com) has been refurbished, with attractive décor and plenty of outside seating... There

Conwy Marina

Conwy quayside

Estuary side footpath

are a few outside tables that have glass windbreaks which are an advantage! Dogs are allowed in this area outside, but not inside. This pub is very popular. Booking is advisable if you are stopping for a meal.

There are some slightly steep inclines on this walk that might make wheelchair access difficult. These are, the pedestrian slope at the start, then as you approach the bridge, and come away from it, and also as you leave the quayside and take the narrow uphill road to join the estuary side path.

(From the Mulberry, it is possible to extend the stroll around the golf course nearby, but the ground is somewhat uneven underfoot, and also very sandy in places, which can make for heavy going! The tide might also affect that stretch.)

Simply of Interest:

Conwy castle was built by Edward 1 of England between 1283 and 1289, as part of his invasion of Wales. It was built as part of a plan to create the walled town of Conwy. It is classed as a World Heritage Site, having eight large towers, and two barbicans. Llywelyn the Great built Aberconwy Abbey in Conwy, but the monks were moved by his troops, to Maenan Abbey, where minimal original remains can be seen.

The beautiful old suspension bridge designed by Thomas Telford, (1826) is open only to pedestrians now.

The smallest house in Britain is found on the quay. It dates back to the 16th century.

Conwy nestles against Conwy Mountain, or "Mynydd y Dref". It is the remains of an ancient volcano that erupted about 450 million years ago.

Stroll No 4

Penrhyn Bay to Angel Bay
to see the grey seals

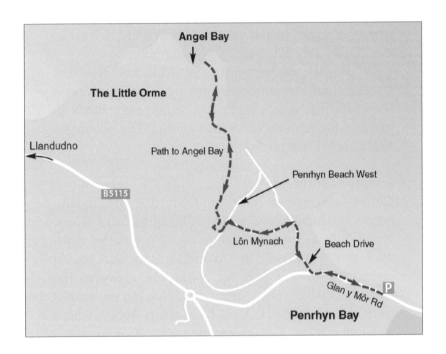

How to get there:

By Car: *Come over the Little Orme from Llandudno, and at the bottom of the hill you will be in Penrhyn Bay. At the roundabout, take the first turning left, which is actually straight on. This is Glan y Môr Rd. Follow this road until the beginning of the promenade, and railings, on your left. There is a hard shoulder lay by at this point. Park here.*

By Bus: *There is a regular bus service from Mostyn St., near M&S in Llandudno, to Penrhyn-side.*

By Train: *There is no railway station nearby.*

Distance: *Approx. 3.5 miles (5.6 kilometres).*

Route of stroll:

Stroll up Glan y Môr Rd., towards the Little Orme, turn right on Beach Drive, then right onto Penrhyn Beach East; continue along here until you reach Lôn Mynach. Turn left up here, and go to the top of this road. At the junction here with Penrhyn Beach West, turn left then immediately right. You will see the entrance to the footpath here. Follow the footpath to Angel Bay.

Comments:

This is a nice stroll, The route is pavement until joining the footpath on Penrhyn Beach West, which is tarmac/concrete, so it flat and not muddy. Even when the path comes to an end, the grass is very short thanks to the rabbits, and is easy to walk on. This is a popular dog walking place. If you intend having a very short stroll from the top end of Penrhyn Beach East, where you can join the path, please be warned, there is a flight

Grey Sealss with pups

Angel Bay

Footpath to Angel Bay

of steps at this point. Do bear in mind that from the start point, on Glan y Môr Rd., the route goes steadily uphill, which might have implications for some Strollers or wheelchair users. The path from Penrhyn Beach West would be manageable for wheelchair users, even though it goes uphill for a short distance.

When you have reached the end of the path, go over to the left near the sign board and look down to the cove. Provided that the tide is not in there will probably be a number of basking grey seals. Even if it is in, you should see some seals in the water, or rolling in the surf perhaps. Do take binoculars with you if possible, as Angel Bay is way below you.

If you do stop for a break at any of the cafés in Rhos-on-Sea on the front, sometimes you can imagine that you are sitting at an outside café on the Mediterranean if you are there on a sunny day, it is very relaxing. Coast café & gift shop (Set back from the road beside The Cayley Flyer Restaurant) is dog friendly, but please check as policies and owners do change.)

Simply of Interest:
Parts of the Little Orme are designated as Sites of Special Scientific Interest. The North Wales Bird Trust is located nearby, and the area is warden patrolled for sea birds.

Grey seals are at Angel Bay all the year round, and January is probably the best time to see them. They might be up to 2.5 metres long, and weigh up to 250 kg. The males tend to be larger than the females. Pups are born in the autumn and early winter, and the mother seal does not feed whilst feeding her pup. She might lose a quarter of her body weight during this time, so becomes very hungry and this will eventually drive her back to the sea. The pups have white fur that is shed quite quickly over about a month, as they learn to fish for themselves.

Stroll No 5

Craig-y-don paddling Pool via the promenade, to Llandudno Pier and back

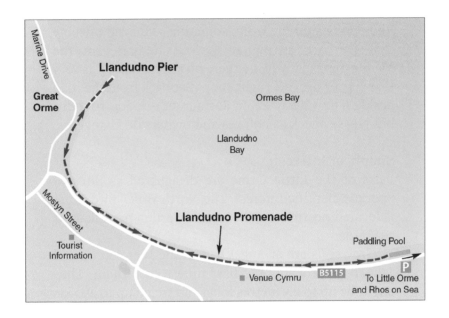

How to get there:

By Car: *Come into Llandudno, and head for the promenade, then turn right towards Craig-y-don Paddling pool which has shelters, café kiosk, WCs, etc. around it, and is easily seen. A lifeboat station is nearby. Park on the road near here. There is no parking fee in this area.*

By Bus: *Arriva runs a bus service between Blaenau Ffestiniog, Betws-y-coed, and Llanrwst to Llandudno. Llew Jones runs a bus service between Betws-y-coed and Llandudno, on the west side of the valley. The X1 bus service on the east side of the valley, runs between Dolwyddelan and Llandudno.*

By Train: *The Arriva train service on the Conwy Valley line runs between Llandudno and Blaenau Ffestiniog.*

Distance: *4 miles (2 miles each way) (3.2 kilometres each way).*

Route of stroll:

From the paddling pool on the promenade in Craig-y-don, to the end of Llandudno prom, then along pier, and back. You might like to call in at any of the cafés on Mostyn Street before returning.

Comments:

This is a good bracing stroll. The promenade is wide and level, if inclined towards the sea slightly. Cyclists are allowed to ride along the prom, but are mindful of pedestrians. The pier is as popular as ever, and has plentiful benches for those of us that wish to take our time and enjoy the atmosphere, sea air and wonderful views. This is a good place to appreciate the beautiful curve of the bay, and all the hotels. There are all sorts of fun attractions for children and families on the

Llandudno Pier

The Promenade, Llandudno

The Great Orme from Craig y Don

approach to the pier. If you need a break before walking back, there is a café on the roundabout just set back from the promenade, and it has outside seating.

Simply of Interest:

Llandudno, the largest seaside resort in Wales, is deemed to be the "Queen of Welsh Resorts", a title it has enjoyed since 1864. Originally the town developed from Stone Age, Bronze Age and Iron Age settlements on the Great Orme. Nowadays, much of the town is owned by Mostyn Estates.

The town takes its name from the ancient parish of Saint Tudno, which encompasses a number of different local townships.

Llandudno has a connection with Alice in Wonderland, as the "real" Alice (Alice Liddell) spent a number of holidays in Llandudno.

The two mile curved Victorian promenade and the hotels between the Great and Little Orme, is a great attraction for visitors, being wide and flat, offering a wonderful view of the pier, and 10 miles out to sea, where "Gwynt y Môr", the second largest off shore wind farm in the world can be seen.

For fishing enthusiasts, who want to fish or go crabbing off the pier, a license is needed from "Pier Point Tackle and Bait" which is based on the pier.

Stroll No 6

Port Eirias/Colwyn Bay Water Sports Centre, on Colwyn Bay Prom, to Rhos-on-Sea

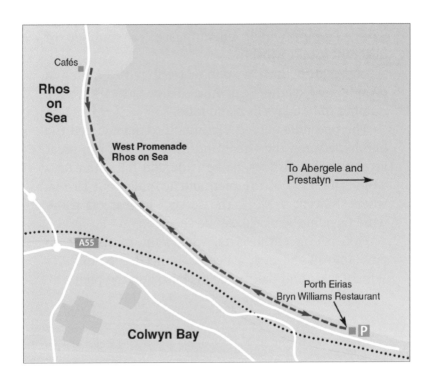

How to get there:

By Car: *Take Junction 20 off the A55, at traffic lights follow signs to Rhos-on-Sea. At The large roundabout take the 4th turning on your left, Whitehall Rd, and follow this to Caley Promenade, turn left and join the main West Promenade Rd. Turn Right here, and go towards the old Colwyn Bay Pier. Just beyond this you will see a modern building on the sea front. This is The Colwyn Bay Water Sports Centre, and Bryn Williams, Porth Eirias Restaurant. Parking is free here.*

By Bus: *There is no easy bus route to Porth Eirias, other than Arriva buses that run between Llandudno and Colwyn Bay, from the Coach park in Llandudno, to the Central Hotel in Colwyn Bay. It is 1.2 miles (1.9 km) from there.*

By Train: *On coming out of Colwyn Bay station, turn left and take the road that leads down to the promenade. Turn right on the prom, and you will see Port Eirias. (Allow 10-15 mins).*

Distance: *Approx. 4 miles (2 miles each way) (approx. 6.4 kilometres total stroll).*

Route of stroll:

On leaving Porth Eirias, turn towards Rhos-on-Sea, and stroll along to the promenade until you reach whichever coffee shop you fancy taking a break at. Return the same way when duly refreshed!

Comments:

This is a very pleasant easy, flat walk, which is suitable for pushchairs, and also wheelchair users, but in view of the slope up to the start of the old pier, and slope down, it would probably be easier for wheelchair users to start the stroll on the west side (i.e. the Rhos-on-Sea side) of the old pier, where there is also parking. Cyclists do use the promenade, so please be aware of this.

If you fancy a coffee or snack before returning to the start point of the stroll, there are several very pleasant cafés on the front in Rhos-on-Sea. Coast café in Rhos-on-Sea allows dogs inside. (Please note that owners and policies do change so it might be advisable to check this if you have a dog.)

View from Rhos-on-Sea

Rhos-on-Sea village

Looking towards Old Colwyn

Simply of Interest:
Bryn Williams Porth Eirias restaurant is a beach front bistro. Colwyn Bay Water sports Centre which is in the same building, offers a blue flag beach, sailing tuition, power boating and hiring facilities to enjoy sailing, windsurfing, kayaking, canoeing, and SUP boarding.

Colwyn Bay has received a gold award 8 times in the Wales in Bloom competition. Eirias Park, a fine sporting and leisure facility is nearby and worth a visit. There are fifty acres of parkland, swimming pool, fitness and health suites. The Eirias Events Centre, the Athletics arena, tennis courts, bowling green, boating lake, and children's playground and picnic area make this Park an ideal place for many to visit. The Welsh Mountain Zoo is a very popular place to visit for families, and offers a delightful and interesting day out (website: welshmountainzoo.org).

St Trillo's chapel in Rhos-on-Sea is a charming tiny 6th century stone built chapel having seating for 6 people. It is situated approx. 100 yds. beyond Rhos point, which if you follow the coastal footpath going west, you cannot miss it. There is also a playground nearby.

Stroll No 7

Llanfairfechan Promenade going west on the coastal path To the Nature reserve and back

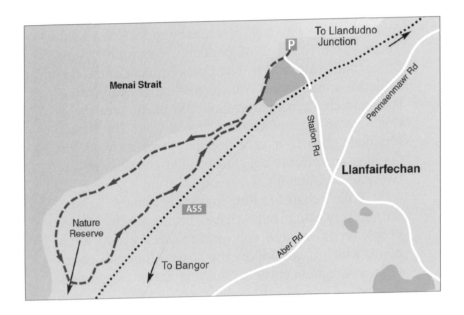

How to get there:

By Car: *Take the A55, and at the roundabout signalling Llanfairfechan, turn off here onto Penmaenmawr Rd, and drive into the town. At the traffic lights on the main street, turn right down Station Road. You will soon reach the promenade where there is a large single many windowed building. This is the Pavilion Café. The car park here is the start point.*

By Bus: *There is a bus service to Llanfairfechan from the coach park in Llandudno.*

By Train: *Llanfairfechan station is on West Shore Rd., Come out of the station and follow the road to the right, keeping on West Shore which goes off to the left slightly. At the end of West shore, turn left onto Caradog Pl. This leads down to the Promenade and the start of the walk.*

Distance: *Approx. 3 miles (4.8 kilometres). However, the coastal path is 870 miles (1,400km) long, so this walk could be as long as you choose.*

Route of stroll:

Follow the coastal path along the promenade, as far as the little nature reserve, where a break can be taken at a convenient picnic bench, before taking a return loop through a wooded area which eventually re-joins the coastal path.

Comments:

This is a particualrly enjoyable walk, with bracing air, amazing views out to Puffin Island and Anglesey. The birdlife is superb. The cygnets on the pond were (in September) developing their adult plumage, and the oyster catchers were in full voice.

Coastal path view, Llanfairfechan

Approaching the nature reserve

The green at the start of the walk

In summer there can be spectacular sunsets, looking out to sea.

The first part of the walk is wide and concreted. It does however become narrower and eventually the path is on flat short grassy ground. It does remain level.

This first section would be suitable for wheelchair users and pushchairs, but once beyond the wide path it would become difficult.

Beyond the Nature reserve, it appears that walkers would be on the somewhat uneven sandy and stony shore line. We have not explored beyond this point, so I do not know how long the " path" is like this for.

There are a couple of cafés near to the start/end of the stroll which will offer refreshment. 'Oceans' – a tapas/seafood restaurant, set back from the promenade, will not disappoint you.

Simply of Interest:

Llanfairfechan is a seaside town with superb views out to Puffin Island and Anglesey. The nature reserve Morfa Madryn is a salt marsh area to the west of the town, where cormorants, shags, and other birds including lapwing, and little egret can be seen.

There is evidence that there was a community in Llanfairfechan from about 7000 years ago, created by people who settled there after the last Ice Age.

It is thought that the original recipe for Guinness might have come from here.

The building of the road, and the railway in 1845 made a great difference to the town, and also the safety for travellers to Anglesey, who had hitherto had to walk along the beach, or over the hills, risking life and limb whilst on their way to Bangor.

Stroll No 8

The River Llugwy, Betws-y-coed riverside walk, and The Golf Course

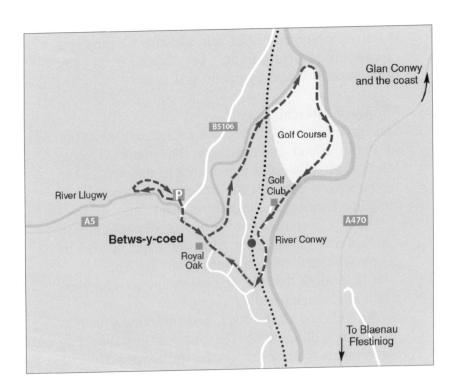

How to get there:

By Car: *From the A470 down the east side of the Conwy Valley, take the A5 into Betws-y-coed, and drive almost through the town, until you reach The Pont y Pair bridge on your right. Go over the bridge and turn immediately left where you will see the Pay and Display car park on your right.*

By Bus: *Llew Jones runs a bus service from Llandudno Coach Park, And the No19 bus runs from outside M&Co on the A546 (Gloddaeth Ave, Llandudno).*

By Train: *Arriva Trains run to Betws-y-coed from Llandudno.*

Distance: *Approx. 3.5 miles (approx. 5.6 kilometres).*

Route of stroll:

From Pont y Pair Pay and Display car park, go into the wooded area, and follow the wooden walkway alongside the river Llugwy. The walkway comes to an end after a while, and becomes a wide flat path to a picnic area. Turn back here and take a left turn on the path where it leads uphill to the road. Turn right onto the road, and return to the bridge. Cross the bridge, and turn left, and walk down the road, turning left opposite the Royal Oak Hotel and go towards the Tourist Information Centre and adjacent businesses. Close to this group of buildings where the TIC is, on the left is a five bar gate. Pass though this gate, (even though it says PRIVATE), and follow the track all the way round the golf course. This runs into Old Church Rd, which leads back to the A5. Turn right on the A5 and return to the car park.

Footpath beside the Conwy

Wooden walkway beside the Llugwy   *Golf Course footpath*

Comments:

A walk with variety, having the woodland and river environment, the wooden walkway, the bustle of the town, then trees and river, and finally back to the town.

Please note that the first part of this walk is the only section that would be suitable for wheelchair users; provided they return along the wooden walkway.

The point where the Llugwy meets the Conwy is lovely. Quite a lot of the path round the golf course is narrow, allowing only single file walking, and in places it is somewhat uneven, and stony, particularly since the floods of the 2015/2016 winter. There are a couple of places where there are one or two earthy "steps", but these are managed quite easily with care. However it is a lovely walk.

If you wish to avoid any slopes, once you reach the picnic area by the river on the first stretch of the walk, do return to the Pont y Pair Bridge the way that you have just come, as the path up to the road, although not long, is a bit steep.

You have a choice of places for that cup of tea and a tasty snack, such as the Garden Nursery on the main road (gardennursery.co.uk) or The Royal Oak Hotel which is 75 yards further up the main road. (royaloakhotel.co.jp).

Simply of Interest:
Betws-y-coed means "Prayer house in the wood". It is a very popular destination for many visitors, having attractive shops, places to eat, and plenty of accommodation. Many keen climbers and hill walkers come to this area, as Snowdonia offers a great variety of outdoor activities for all ages.

The Waterloo Bridge was built by Thomas Telford, and this not only facilitated good connection between London and Holyhead, but also brought greater development to the area.

The Swallow Falls, which are about 2 miles out of Betws-y-coed on the A5, are definitely worth a visit especially after heavy rain! Please be warned as there are a lot of steps down to the water's edge viewing point.

Stroll No 9

The River Conwy, Trefriw to Llanrwst and back

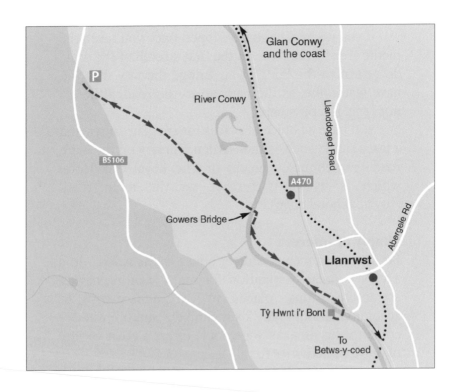

How to get there:

By Car: *Trefriw lies on the east side of the Conwy Valley, on the B5106 which runs between Betws-y-coed and Conwy. This road can be accessed from the A470 by going over Pont Fawr bridge in Llanrwst, or the bridge at Tal-y-cafn. Once in Trefriw, you will find the car park is opposite the Trefriw Woollen Mills.*

By Bus: *Llew Jones runs a No 19 bus service between Llandudno and Betws-y-coed, down the east side of the valley. (llewjonesinternational.co.uk)*

By Train: *There is no railway station in Trefriw.*

Distance: *Approx. 3.5 miles (5.6 kilometres) there and back.*

Route of stroll:

From Trefriw car park, follow the track away from the town. This takes you to Gower's Bridge (pedestrian). At this point wheelchair users would need to turn back (unless they wanted to continue on the track ahead to Llanrwst.)

Cross the bridge, then turn immediately right, passing through a gate, and follow a path along the riverside. This leads you into Llanrwst, to Pont Fawr bridge. At this point there is a flight of some stone steps to take you up to the road. Turn right, and walk over the bridge to Tu Hwnt i'r Bont for a coffee stop. When you are revitalised, return the way that you came.

Comments:

This is a country stroll with a balance between tarmac track and grassy riverside path. The latter can be a bit uneven in places, and it would be best done on a dry day!

Towards the end of the stroll, as you come into Llanrwst, is where the path becomes a wooden walkway, for a stretch. The very final section is stone/slate. Take care as you go over the bridge to Tu Hwnt i'r Bont, as it is narrow, and there is no pavement. If you wish to have your coffee etc. outside,

Tu Hwnt i'r Bont Tea Room

Footpath alongside the river Conwy

Gowers bridge

you will need to go to the rear of the building for service.

Only the first half of this walk, i.e. as far as Gower's Bridge would be suitable for wheelchair users and pushchairs.

Simply of Interest:

Trefriw sits largely within the Snowdonia National Park, lying on the western slopes of the Conwy valley, which is glaciated. The river Crafnant flows through the village, providing power for the Woolen Mill.

The village is not only known as an ideal starting place for many walks, as the annual Trefriw Walking Festival indicates, but also for the nearby Chalybeate Spa, which was used by the Romans. The waters were one of a few in Europe to have been recognised as having medicinal properties because of the high iron content.

Gower's Bridge was originally a toll bridge. There used to be a house on the Llanrwst side of the bridge where tolls were paid.

Llanrwst has always been a market town, originally developed around the wool trade, but was also renowned for harp and clock manufacture. There are several antique shops to be found in the town today.

Tu Hwnt i'r Bont was originally a courthouse in the 15th century.

St Crwst Church (reached off the square in the town) is on the site of the original 12th century church, which was a thatched wooden building. It has undergone several phases of rebuilding and renovation since then. A beautiful 15th century rood screen can be seen in the church.

Stroll No 10

The River Glaslyn, Beddgelert

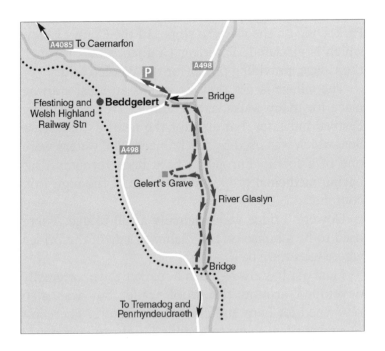

How to get there:

By Car: *Take the A5 out of Betws-y-coed to Capel Curig, and turn left here on the A4086. When you reach the Penygwryd Hotel, continue straight ahead, this is the A498. Do not turn right up to Pen y Pass. You will pass Llyn Gwynant, and Llyn Dinas, and you will eventually reach Beddgelert. (It takes approx 20 mins by car from Capel Curig).*

In the centre of Beddgelert, do not go over the bridge, but drive straight ahead to a free car park only some 120 or so yards ahead on the right. This is a good place to start from.

By Bus: *The Snowdon Sherpa bus between Caernarfon and Porthmadog does stop at Beddgelert.*

By Train: *The Welsh Highland Railway runs a (tourist) service beween Caernarfon and Beddgelert. For further information, please see their website (festrail.co.uk) or call 01766 516024.*

Distance: *2.5 – 3 miles from and back to the car park (4 – 4.8 kilometres).*

Route of stroll:

Return to the bridge by the Tanronnen Pub in Beddgelert, and cross over it, turning left on the other side. Continue for about 60 yds and cross over a narrow footbridge and turn immediately right. Follow the footpath, eventually you will see another footbridge that spans the river, you can cross the bridge and return on the other side of the river, visiting Gelerts grave, and the ruin of the family home, on your way; returning to the riverside footpath back into the village, then back to the car park.

The river Glaslyn

Footpath alongside the Glaslyn

West Highland Railway steam train

Comments:

This is another very pretty walk. Take care on the further section of this walk if you go beyond the second bridge, where the flat topped stone path become rather more uneven, with standing water around the stones, walking becomes more difficult. Turning back after a while is possibly a good idea!

Do not be alarmed if a steam train suddenly appears nearby! You may find that on your return you will be walking in a field with cattle. They are used to walkers, but keeping your dog on a lead would be adviseable. There are plenty of places to find a snack and tea/coffee in Beddgelert. Hebog café on your way back to the car park has outdoor riverside seating. (hebog-beddgelert.co.uk)

If you wish to add another loop to your stroll, and can manage steps and slopes, it is fun to visit the charming little Beddgelert station to see the steam trains. You can check beforehand when they are due by contacting the West Highland Railway. (01766 516024 or see festrail.co.uk)

Simply of Interest:
Beddgelert (bedd: grave) is situated where the river Colwyn meets The river Glaslyn. This is a particularly beautiful area. Moel Hebog rises to the west of the village, and Snowdon is only 5 miles away.

There is a legend about a dog that belonged to Llywelyn the Great., who returns from a hunting trip to find his baby missing, the cradle overturned, and the dog with blood around his jaws. Llywelyn kills the dog then hears the baby cry, from the safety of the upturned cradle. He then sees the dead wolf. Llywelyn is overcome with remorse and guilt, and buries the dog in a ceremonial way. It is said that Llywelyn never smiled again. However it is thought that the origin of the place name is more likely to be associated with an early Christian missionary called Celert or Cilert.

The Church of St Mary at the end of Stryd yr Eglwys stands on the site of a Benedictine monastery. There are parts that date back to the 12th century. The surrounding hillsides of this town are covered in rhododendron in May and June, which is unfortunately severely limiting local natural flora growth. Efforts are being made to curb this growth spread, by cutting and burning.

Stroll No 11

Llangollen Canal

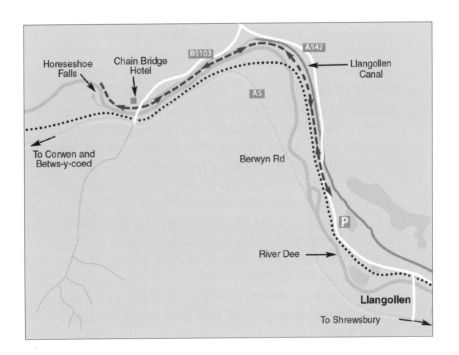

How to get there:

By Car: *From Llanrwst, take the A470 to Betws-y-coed, then the A5 all the way to Llangollen, passing through Pentrefoelas, Cerrigydrudion, and Corwen. At the traffic lights in Llangollen, turn left down Castle St, and go over the bridge, and turn left onto the A542. Follow this road for a short distance and you will see the Pavilion Pay and Display car park on your right.*

By Bus: *There are bus services to and fro from Wrexham, Corwen and Llandudno from Llangollen. A Saturday only service to Llanrwst is operated by Llew Jones.*

By Train: *The Llangollen Railway, is a steam hauled heritage Railway, running between Llangollen and Corwen. There is no regular rail service to Llangollen.*

Distance: *Approx. 4 miles (approx. 6.4 kilometres).*

Route of stroll:

Walk up to the rear left hand corner of the car park, and this will take you directly onto the tarmac canal side path. Turn left onto the path, for a quiet and beautiful stroll up to the Horseshoe Falls. You will pass behind the Chain Bridge Hotel, (chainbridgehotel.com) and will soon reach the Pump House at the end/beginning of the canal. Pass through a gate and walk onto a sheep nibbled grassy meadow by The Horseshoe Falls. You can extend your stroll a little by following the "path" from the meadow here, up to the delightful old Llantysilio church. Return the same way that you came.

Comments:

This is a very pleasant walk. The towpath alongside the canal is flat, and not muddy. You may see Kayakers,

The Horseshoe Falls

Llangollen canal

Llantysilio Parish Church

and white water rafters out on the River Dee, and
sometimes school children have fun canoeing sessions,
on the canal. The Horseshoe Falls is beautiful, being a
low curved waterfall with a wide bay.

The Chain Bridge Hotel sits right on the edge of

the river, with a charming pedestrian bridge that spans the river. The restaurant and bar have superb views of this white water stretch. It is dog friendly, but please check as policies and owners do change.

Simply of Interest:
The Horseshoe Falls is a weir, which is 460 feet long. It was designed by Thomas Telford, and was built to collect water to feed the Llangollen Canal, in 1804.

The weir has been vital in the maintaining of the canal, when much of the Shropshire Union system was closed in 1944. The Horseshoe Falls has been an important source of water to the system. It was taken over by British Waterways in 1948. This stretch of the canal is not navigable by powered boats, as it is too narrow for them to turn around.

Llangollen in Welsh means "a religious settlement". Saint Collen was a 6th century monk who founded a church near the river.

The annual International Music Eisteddfod, a six day event, brings competitors and visitors from all over the world to the area. An *Eisteddfod* is a Welsh cultural event which traditionally includes musical, craft and literary competitions. The International Eisteddfod was started in Llangollen to promote peace, tolerance and understanding between countries after World War II and every country is encouraged to promote its own national language, culture and costumes. It is a lively and colourful week!

Stroll No 12

The River Lledr, Dolwyddelan

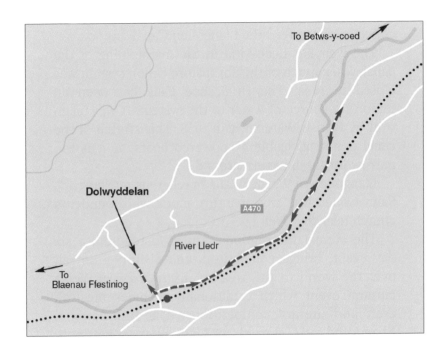

How to get there:

By Car: *Take the A470 going south from the North Wales coast. Pass through Llanrwst, and ignore the turning for Betws-y-coed, and remain on the A470. After about 6 miles from Betws-y-coed, you will reach Dolwyddelan. Turn left at the Spar supermarket, and park opposite the church approx 75yds down the road, where the road is wide.*

By Bus: *Express Motors and Llew Jones run a bus service between Llandudno and Blaenau Ffestiniog.*

By Train: *There is an Arriva trains Wales service between Llandudno Junction and Dolwyddelan.*

Distance: *2.3 miles (3.7 kilometres), but the path to Pont y Pant is approx. 3 miles (4.8 kilometres).*

Route of stroll:

Turn away from the main road, pass over the bridge that crosses the river Lledr, and follow the path to the left which leads past the station on your right, and primary school on your left. The route leads across open land at times, but it remains fairly even and the grass is short. After approx. 1 mile, you will reach a railway bridge, (see photo) the path climbs up quite steeply for about 20 yards. It is also uneven at this point, you can turn back here.

Comments:

This stroll is beside a beautiful stretch of the river Lledr, and is a short one if you are avoiding slopes, but can be extended by just going further. The ground varies from a hard beaten track that is fairly even, to close nibbled grass. There are gentle undulations, but no steep hills until the suggested turnaround point which is at the railway bridge (see photo) where the track becomes stony, and does go uphill. Elen's Castle Hotel in Dolwyddelan opens in the evening, and is dog friendly, but please check, as owners and policies do change (hotelscombined.co.uk).

The River Lledr

Dolwyddelan

Saint Gwyddelan's Church gate

Simply of Interest:

Dolwyddelan means "Gwyddelan's meadow". Gwyddelan was a Celtic missionary, after whom the local church was named. The church is worth visiting, being a grade 1 listed building, with a fine roof, and barrel vaulted chancel. Wooden parts inside the church date back to the early 18th century, but a bronze hand bell that hangs in the church has been dated to 800AD.

The river Lledr is a major tributary of the river Conwy, and it runs along the Lledr Valley from the Crimea Pass near Blaenau Ffestiniog, to Betws-y-coed.

Elen's Castle Hotel in Dolwyddelan, is reputed to be over 300 years old, and was the home of Baron Gwydir. It was sold to his gamekeeper, who turned it into a coaching inn for those keen on hunting.

Dolwyddelan Castle, built by Llywelyn the Great (1173–1240) is considered to be a "masterpiece". It has had a number of additions and refurbishments over the years, the latest of which was completed by the Victorians.

Stroll No 13

Capel Curig, (Siabod Café to Plas y Brenin)

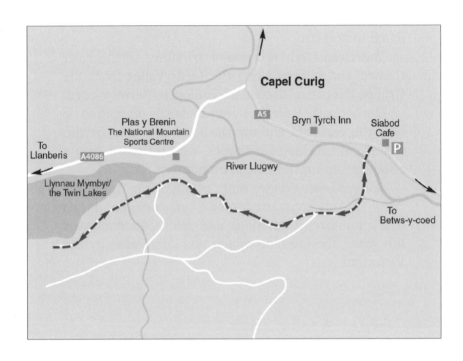

How to get there:

By Car: *Take the A5 from Betws-y-coed towards Capel Curig. Pass the Ty'n y Coed Hotel, and Cobdens Hotel, and approx 1 mile further ahead on the right, is Siabod Café. Park here.*

By Bus: *Express Motors and Llew Jones Coaches run bus services between Llanrwst and Llanberis.*

By Train: *There is no railway station in Capel Curig.*

Distance: *Approx 3.5 miles (approx 5.6 kilometres).*

Route of stroll:

Come out of Siabod Café car park, cross the road, and pass over the bridge that spans the river Llugwy. Follow the woodland track, taking the right fork after about 150 -20080yds, and again later on do not take a left fork, go straight ahead. Pass through two gates, and eventually you will be opposite Plas y Brenin, the National Mountain Sports Centre. Pause here for the views from the pedestrian bridge, then return to the track and continue walking in the same direction until it becomes less easy! The track does get rather boggy, and less even after a while. Return the same way, and enjoy a break at the Siabod Café.
(moelsiabodcafe.co.uk)

Comments:

Of all the walks in this book, this possibly has the steepest short "hill". As soon as you cross the bridge at the beginning of the walk, the track gradually pulls up for approx 100 yards, then goes downhill for about 80 yards. It then is fairly flat, with occasional undulations.

Twin Lakes, and bridge to Plas y Brenin

The ski slope, rear of Plas y Brenin   *The woodland track*

The surface is hard, compacted shale and gravel, with occasional potholes!

This is however, a lovely woodland and riverside walk, and is particularly beautiful in mid-May when the bluebells are out.

If you stand on the narrow bridge when you reach Plas y Brenin, look across the lake and you might see Snowdon on a clear day. It is also fun to watch the groups of children and young people having canoeing or kayaking sessions on the lake. Dogs are allowed into Siabod café, but it is always worth checking as owners and policies do change.(moelsiabodcafe.co.uk)

Simply of Interest:
Plas y Brenin offers mountain leadership qualifications, and also kayaking, walking, climbing, and canoeing courses and holidays. There is also an indoor climbing wall.

Snowdon (Yr Wyddfa in Welsh) is the highest mountain in Wales. It is 1,085 metres high (3,560ft) and was created by volcanic activity, with glaciation forming the peak and also the ridge of Crib Goch. There are six main routes to the summit, and there is a rack and pinion railway from Llanberis that operates from Whitsun to October. (snowdon railway.co.uk)

The mountain is renowned for its wild flowers, in particular the Snowdon Lily. It has a rich mix of habitats, that sustain a huge variety of plants, including lichens and and freshwater algae to vascular plants.

Along with Scafell Pike, and Ben Nevis, Snowdon makes up the National Three peaks Challenge.

Stroll No 14

Bryn Glo café car park, Capel Curig, to Tŷ Hyll, Betws-y-coed

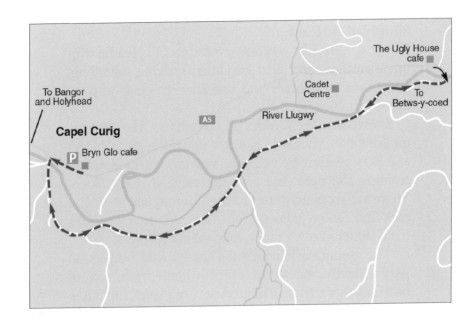

How to get there:

By Car: *Take the A5 through Betws-y-coed towards Capel Curig. Just as you pass the road sign saying Capel Curig, the road takes a gradual bend to the right. Approx. 50 yds. ahead on your right is the Bryn Glo café and the adjacent car park. This is free and quite spacious. Park here.*

By Bus: *There is a bus service on the A5, and there is a stop/coach station at Cyfyng Falls near the bridge.*

By Train: *There is no rail service in this area.*

Distance: *Approx. 5 miles there and back (8 kilometres).*

Route of stroll:

Leave the Bryn Glo car park, cross the road diagonally to the right and follow the pavement to the stone bridge. Enjoy the sight of the river (Cyfyng Falls) tumbling over and between massive rocks. Follow this quiet and narrow road over the bridge, and all the way to re-join the A5. Do not take any tracks off it. Once at the A5 you can take a breather at Tŷ Hyll café, (theuglyhouse.co.uk) which is off to your left, but take care as there is no pavement here. When revived, return the way that you came.

Comments:

This is the longest stroll in this book, but it is very pretty, as the route dips into the shade of woodland from time to time, then out through more open sheep farming land. Babbling streams here and there add to the beauty. There is an early "hill"(downwards), but essentially this is an undulating and steady downhill walk, so you will notice that when you return the same

Tŷ Hyll

Track to Tŷ Hyll

Cyfyng Falls

way, that you are going slightly uphill. Traffic along this road is minimal.

Simply of Interest:

Capel Curig is situated in Snowdonia, and is a particularly popular hill and mountain walking area. Moel Siabod (872 metres) which is nearby, is enjoyed by many visitors. Snowdonia rocks are very old, going back as far as 625 million years, to the Precambrian period. North Wales does experience very small earthquake tremors from time to time.

The A5 road runs through Capel Curig, and this is the main Trunk road from Marble Arch in London to Admiralty Arch in Holyhead. The section that was originally built by the Romans and named Watling Street lies between London and Shrewsbury.

Tŷ Hyll possibly goes back as the 15th century. In Welsh, 'hyll' can mean 'rugged' as well as ugly. It is built of huge rugged stones, and some claim that it was not only built overnight, but it was created by ugly people... namely robbers and thieves who stole from travellers on the road. Today it is a popular tearoom. If you plan to call there to break your walk, it might be advisable to check that they are open if you are calling out of season.

The owners also breed honey bee queens, and bees for local beekeepers, and you can visit the honey bee room upstairs to find out more about their work. (theuglyhouse.co.uk).

Stroll No 15

Dyserth to Meliden

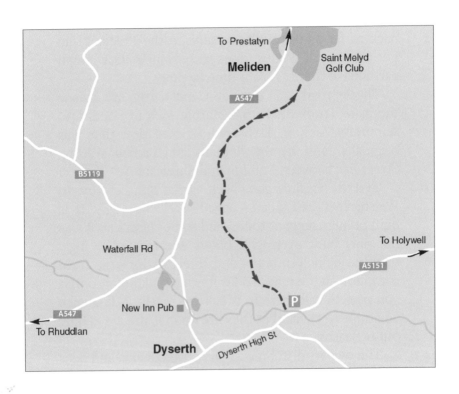

How to get there:

By Car: *Take the A55 to junction 24, where you turn off, and at the roundabout here, take the turn for the A547. This will take you almost all the way via Rhuddlan. Outside Rhuddlan you will pass Voel coaches on your right. Soon you will come to a junction with the B5119, turn right here. This is Waterfall Rd. Continue past The New Inn pub which will be on your right, opposite a church and churchyard; Turn left at the traffic lights, and go up the High Street in Dyserth. Follow the road which later veers to the left then begins to go quite steeply downhill. Look out for a yellow steel framed entrance to a car park very soon on your left. Park here.*

By Bus: *There are bus services between Rhyl, and also Prestatyn, and Dyserth.*

By Train: *There is no station in Dyserth.*

Distance: *3 miles (approx. 4.8 kilometres) as a there and back 1.5 mile walk, but this Dyserth to Prestatyn walkway is 2.5 miles long, so the walk could be extended.*

Route of stroll:

Having parked as above, enter the walkway which leads off to the left. Remain on this wide footpath, until you reach Meliden, where there is a narrow tarmac path and gateway off to your left. Return the same way. If you fancy a pub snack when you get back to Dyserth, you could call at the New Inn Pub (also sign boarded as Y Dafarn Newydd) on Waterfall Rd. (thenewinndyserth.co.uk)

Comments:

There are some good benches along this totally flat surfaced track, certainly for the first half mile, so anyone that wants only a very short walk; I suggest you bring your crossword or book and relax in the dappled shade. There is the occasional cyclist, or jogger that comes by, and regular dog walkers.

You will notice perhaps, that as you walk back to the start point, that you will be going slightly uphill. This stretch is particularly beautiful in June when the wild flowers are at their best.

The track from Dyserth to Meliden

Bridge that once spanned the railway

View looking towards Prestatyn

Simply of Interest:

The pearl bordered fritillary butterfly, the lesser horseshoe bat, white violets and orchids are among the rare treasures that might be seen in this area. The hills here are part of the Clwydian Range, which is predominantly carboniferous limestone. Consequently, "Meliden Mountain" is a Site of Special Scientific Interest. This area also has great amount of archaeological and historic interest. Talargoch mines that were thought to be Roman, extracted lead and silver. Zinc was also mined later on.

Both Dyserth and Meliden are mentioned in the Domesday Book of 1086. The local church in Dyserth dates back to the 16th century. There is a stunning waterfall nearby but please note that there is an entrance fee to see it.

The village of Meliden also grew because of the mining and quarrying in the area. Its little church sits on the site of what was presumably a timber one in 1086. There are several interesting historical features, one of which is the burial register which shows many entries for sailors that drowned off the nearby coast, a number of them were unknown.

Stroll No 16

"Shore to Shore", Llandudno

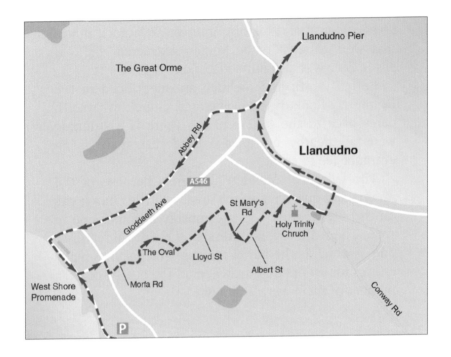

How to get there:

By Car: *Come into Llandudno via Deganwy on the A546, and just past the turning to Llandudno hospital, there is a roundabout. Go up over the bridge, and follow this road to the end where there is a small roundabout at West Shore, at the junction of Gloddaeth Ave., turn left here, and left again. The Pay and Display car park at the far end, by the Beach Café, is the start point. Parking is however free on this street.*

By Bus: *Arriva buses run from the Palladium in Llandudno to West Shore, and Sapphire buses run from Rhyl.*

By Train: *There is no railway station at West Shore.*

Distance: *3.4 miles.*

Route of stroll:

Walk east along the West Shore prom, as far as Gloddaeth Ave, turn right at the roundabout, and opposite the shops take the first turning on your left, into Morfa Rd. continue to the end of this road, and take the narrow ginnel through to The Oval where you will turn left. Walk across to Lloyd St, right onto St Mary's Rd, left onto Albert St., then to Trinity Square. You will see the church here.

From here walk to the right along Mostyn St., as far as the pedestrian crossing, and head towards the Promenade. The Imperial hotel (theimperial.co.uk) will be on your left as you reach Mostyn Crescent, the main street along the front. The Imperial Hotel will be on your left. Stop here for amazing scones! Continue the walk along the prom, onto the pier, back, and up Church walks, then down Abbey Road, back to West Shore, where you can revive yourself once again at the Beach Café. (westshorebeachcafe.com).

Llandudno Pier

Low tide at West Shore   *The boating pool West Shore*

Comments:

As this is a town walk, it is not muddy. The stretch up Church walks is the only uphill section, which is about 150 yards. Enjoy the Victorian architecture, bijou gardens, and seeing parts of this town that are not often seen. The different sea views from both West shore, and the North Shore are interesting. From the

West Shore you can look out towards Puffin Island and Anglesey, and from the North Shore you will see "Gwynt y Môr" (Sea Wind) the second largest off shore windfarm in the World. West Shore is inclined to be breezier, and so attracts wind surfers, which are fun to watch. If you have a dog, you can sit outside on the terrace at The Imperial Hotel, and also the Beach Café.

Simply of Interest:
The town of Llandudno developed from the Stone, Bronze, and Iron Ages. The Copper Mine on the Great Orme is a fascinating place to visit to learn more about the ancient history of the area, with regard to mining.

Much of the town is owned by Mostyn Estates, and it is home to a number of wild Kashmiri goats that have descended from a few goats given to Lord Mostyn by Queen Victoria. The area is a famous for its flora and fauna, and wide variety of sea birds.

The Great Orme Tram, and The Llandudno Cable Car, the Pier, and attractive wide main shopping street, are but a few of the attractions that make Llandudno a popular place to stay.

The first footpath around the Great Orme was built in 1858, and in 1872 it was partially upgraded to be able to take carriages, and the work was completed in 1878. The circular walk all round the Great Orme, returning to your start point, is approx. 5.5miles. (8.8 kilometres)

Stroll No 17

Llyn Crafnant (Crafnant Lake)

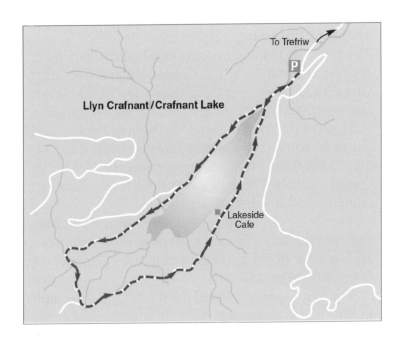

How to get there:

By Car: *From the B5106 that runs down the west side of the Conwy Valley, stop in Trefriw, and take the steep hill to the side of Trefriw Woollen Mills, veering right where the road divides early on. Follow this narrow road for approx. 2 miles until you reach the Crafnant Lake Pay and Display car park on your right. Park here.*

By Bus: *There is no bus service up to the lake.*

By Train: *There is no station nearby.*

Distance: *Approx. 3 miles (approx. 4.8 kilometres).*

Route of stroll:

On leaving the car park, turn right and stroll uphill towards the lake. When you reach it, go through the gate on your right, and follow the wide track all the way round. At the far end of the lake it is a little more uneven, and there is a gradual downward hill (not very steep) of approx. 100 yds. You will turn left through a gate shortly after this point, to go along the near side of the lake. There are one or two uphill slopes on this stretch, before it flattens out as you pass the café on the way back to the car park.

Comments:

The narrow road up to the lake does have a number of passing places for oncoming vehicles, but be prepared to have to reverse into these if there is oncoming traffic.

There are toilets in the car park. This is a good walk, and it is essentially flat with a slight downward incline at the far end of the lake. There are a few places

Llyn Crafnant

The track round Llyn Crafnant

The lakeside café

where winter storms have affected the track surface, but on the whole it is sound. The Lakeside Café has a good menu. But if you want to be sure that they are open when you have walked round the lake, and really need that coffee and a bite to eat, do check beforehand as they do close at certain times. (llyn-crafnant.co.uk). Dogs need to be on a lead for the "return" stretch of this walk, because of the sheep that occasionally roam freely. For anyone wanting a shorter stroll, with a stop half way; I suggest going up the left hand side of the lake as far as the café, and back. This might be only a little more than half a mile each way.

Simply of Interest:

Llyn Crafnant is a particularly beautiful lake, that is about one mile long, spreading to 63 acres, and has a depth of 71ft. Gwydir Forest with its biking and walking trails, lies to the north; and the surrounding hills and crags of Snowdonia make for superb views all the way round. The name Crafnant has been taken from the old Welsh word "craf" meaning garlic, and "nant" which means stream. Llyn Crafnant is but one of numerous lakes in Gwydir Forest.

Fishermen enjoy fishing this lake for brown trout and rainbow trout, and it is possible to hire boats at the lakeside café for this purpose, or for pleasure.

Afon Crafnant flows from the lake down to Trefriw. This water is partially diverted to generate electricity for the Trefriw Woollen Mills, where beautiful Welsh tapestry bedspreads, tweeds and rugs are woven from raw wool. It is possible to see some products being woven, and also some of the other working machinery. (t-w-m.co.uk)

Stroll No 18

Llyn Brenig

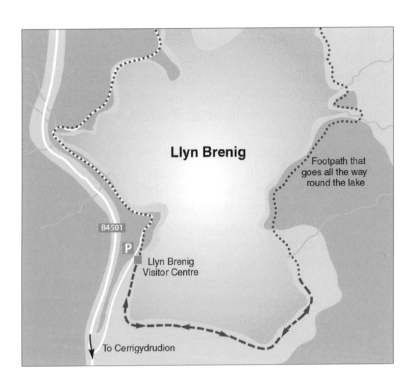

How to get there:

By Car: *Take the A470 going south. At Betws-y-coed, where the Waterloo Bridge is on your right, do not turn into the town, but veer left, taking the A5. Continue through Pentrefoelas, to Cerrigydrudion, where you turn off to the left, and taking the left fork (straight ahead) in the road that runs past the front of the hotel onto the B4501, and follow the signs for Llyn Brenig. Park in the Visitor Centre Car Park.*

By Bus: *There are bus services between Llyn Brenig and Corwen and also between Rhyl and Llyn Brenig. The bus takes passengers right to the visitor centre by the lake.*

By Train: *There is no train service that will take you to Llyn Brenig.*

Distance: *3 – 4 miles (4.8 – 6.4 kilometres) suggested distance; but it is possible to walk round the lake which is 9 miles (14.5 kilometres).*

Route of stroll:

Park in the Visitor Centre car park and take the footpath down towards the lake and follow it round onto the dam, and veering left to the far side of the lake. Turn back when you need to.

Comments:

Llyn Brenig is a centre for outdoor activities, including walking, cycling, fishing and sailing. It offers you an open, sometimes windy and wild atmospheric experience! It can be exhilarating and yet so relaxing as there is minimal other habitation to be seen. The bleating of sheep, and the call of the birds makes you feel very close to nature. Do look out for ospreys...

There is also an adventure playground for children.

Our last visit was in horizontal sleet, but we loved it. The track round the lake is wide, sound, and even. There are stretches if you are going all the way round, where the route is shared with the road.

Llyn Brenig Visitor Centre

Footpath towards the dam

Llyn Brenig and track over the dam

Simply of Interest:

Llyn Brenig sits at 1,200 feet up on the Denbigh Moors, set in the middle of the Hiraethog Mountains. Its purpose is to regulate the water flow in the river Dee which supplies North East Wales and North West England.

During construction of the lake some Bronze Age artefacts were discovered, and also a camp used by Mesolithic hunter/gatherers. There are some archaeological trails around the lake, including a ring cairn. Further information can be obtained at the café.

It is possible to enjoy sailing, fishing, and canoeing on the lake, but the only power craft allowed are those used by fishermen, (particularly fly fishing) and the sailing club.

The visitor centre does provide café facilities, fishing licences, and bike hire. (Llyn-brenig.co.uk) Enjoy!

Stroll No 19

Ysbyty Ifan and a drovers route in Pentrefoelas

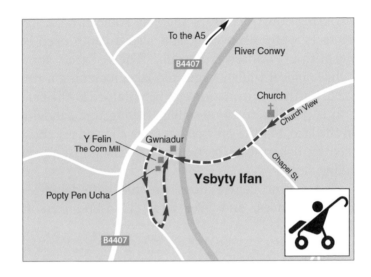

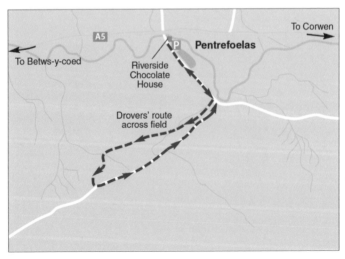

How to get there:

By Car: *Take the A470 to Betws-y-coed, then the A5 going south. Pass through a winding, bendy stretch of road known locally as "The Padog Bends". The road eventually straightens out. Take the right turn soon on the B4407 to Ysbyty Ifan, and park near the church where the road is wider.*

By Bus: *There is a bus service between Llanrwst and Ysbyty Ifan, and also between Cerrigydrudion and Ysbyty Ifan.*

By Train: *There is no main line station in Ysbyty Ifan.*

Distance: *.5 mile (0.8 kilometres) in Ysbyty Ifan, then 1.5 miles in Pentrefoelas.*

Route of stroll: (in Ysbyty Ifan)
Stroll down the hill, over the bridge and visit the Corn Mill, then following the lane in front of the houses by the river, take a short circuit back to the Mill, and walk back uphill, to visit the church, and finally returning to the start point.

Drive back to the A470, and turn right. In Pentrefoelas, turn right opposite the Foelas Arms Hotel and park at The Riverside Chocolate House. Ready for the second part of the stroll.

Route of stroll: (from the Riverside Chocolate House)
Leave the car park, turning left onto the pavement, walking towards the primary school, and going gently uphill. Continue past the school to the road junction and just past a five bar gate is the entrance to the drover's route. Take this track, and follow it through another five bar gate until it reaches a quiet road. Turn left onto the road, then left at the junction where you left the road earlier on. Return to the start point along the pavement.

The bridge at Ysbyty Ifan

The Corn Mill

The track, Pentrefoelas

Comments:

This is a delightful way to spend a little time. Ysbyty Ifan sits on a hillside so the road down to the bridge is quite a steep slope. Pause there to enjoy the river Conwy, which is not much more than a busy stream at this point as it rises near here.

On Thursdays, the Post Office is open all day in the large house by the river, next to the post box. The post mistress holds the key to the Corn Mill, and will open it for you. Not only is it a beautiful old building, but it is also used for storage purposes by local small businesses. Some of the craft work there is lovely.

The route from The Riverside Chocolate House is partly on pavement, then the field track (Drover's track) is inclined uphill and although hard beaten ground it is somewhat uneven underfoot. There are deep ruts here and there, and this could be difficult going particularly in bad weather! The final stretch is on a quiet tarmac road. When leaving the Drover's track, and joining the road look back to see the Snowdon Horseshoe.

Simply of Interest:
In 1951, Lord Penrhyn died, and in lieu of death duties, the village was transferred from the Treasury to The National Trust. The estate covers over 20,000 acres covering a huge stretch of mountainous land and three valleys, all of which falls within The Snowdonia National Park.

Tŷ Mawr Wybrnant is a 16th century farmhouse in the vicinity, where Bishop William Morgan was born. He translated the Bible into Welsh and it was published in 1588, establishing a new modern prose style for the old language.

The Knights of St John, the Order of Hospitallers set up a hospital in the late 12th century, to care for pilgrims. Ysbyty Ifan means Hospital of St John, but it was abolished in 1540 during the Dissolution of the Monasteries. The church of St John is built on the site of the old hospital.

The Corn Mill and its pitchback waterwheel, was built by the Penrhyn Estate in 1870. Corn grinding ceased in the early 1940's, and it later was converted to generate electricity for two decades, but this function ceased some while ago. It is owned by the National Trust.

Stroll No 20

Lôn Las Menai, Caernarfon

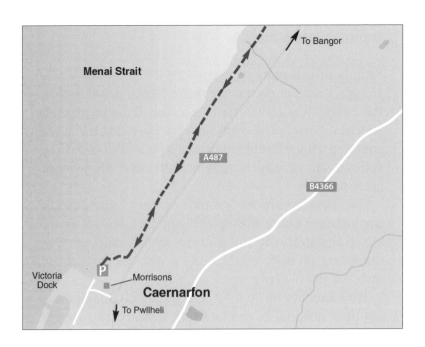

How to get there:

By Car: *Leave the A55 at junction 9, taking the A487 south west to Caernarfon. Pass through Y Felinheli and continue on this road to Caernarfon. Alternatively take the A5 through Capel Curig and Bethesda which joins the A55 at junction 11. Stay on the A55 going towards Anglesey, and leave at junction 9, Pick up the A487 to Caernarfon as above.*

By Bus: *Arriva buses run a service between Llandudno, Bangor and Caernarfon. Clynnog and Trefor buses, and Express Motors run between Pwllheli and Caernarfon.*

By Train: *There is no railway or station in Caernarfon.*

Distance: *Flexible.*

Route of stroll:

Starting from the lower car park from behind Morrisons supermarket, join the Lôn Las Menai walk for as long as is comfortable before turning back. (After a few miles the path actually joins the main road for a period.) A nice place to visit for a snack and browse afterwards is Fron Goch Garden Centre only 6 mins drive away. (frongoch-gardencentre.co.uk)

Directions to Fron Goch Garden Centre

After the walk, leave car park and return to roundabout. Turn Rt here onto 487 Pwllheli Rd. Pass Tesco on Rt. Go straight over roundabout. Very soon after this take the first turning to the right. This is Pant Rd, The road forks almost immediately. Keep to the left. Do not go up Coed Helen Rd! The Fron Goch Garden Nursery will be down this lane on your left. (About 1 mile from the 487).

The Lôn Las Menai track

The start of the walk

Menai Strait and Anglesey

Comments:

There is a lovely view of the Menai Strait and over to Anglesey, at the outset. This is a nice flat tarmac stroll through broad leaf woodland, and has only one slight "dip" in it. It was originally the railway route between Bangor and Caernarfon, now used by cyclists as well as walkers. The footpath does narrow a bit in places, but it would still be fine for wheelchair users and pushchairs/strollers.

Simply of Interest:
Caernarfon is a Royal town. Edward 1 completed his invasion of Wales in 1283 by securing a chain of castles and walled towns; Caernarfon castle being started at the end of the campaign. The castle and the colonial town built in its shadow, offering its many privileged rights to the settlers at the expense of the native population, was much hated by the Welsh who rebelled and destroyed it in 1295 under Madog ap Llywelyn and 1403 under Owain Glyndŵr.

Caernarfon's history has made it a popular tourist attraction. The medieval town walls are themselves of interest, forming a 730 metre circle around the old town. The church of St Peblig dates back to the 14th century, being built upon a Roman Mithraeum.

The Menai Strait is a narrow strip of water separating Anglesey from the Welsh mainland. Thomas Telford built the iron suspension bridge which carries the A5 to Anglesey. The Strait is a hazardous stretch of water because of tides, shifting sand, currents, rocks and whirlpools!

Anglesey is where the village is that has the very long name:
Llanfairpwllgwyngyllgogerychwyrndrobwllllantysilio-gogogoch, meaning in English:

"The church of St Mary in a hollow of white hazel near a rapid whirlpool and near St. Tysilio's church by the red cave".

Best Walks in Wales

A series of guide books to take you to every corner of this magnificent walking country

- Short family walks
- Excellent coastal walks
- Hill and mountain walks & panoramic views
- Level lakeside and valley walks
- Woodland and nature walks
- Fascinating heritage and history guides
- Clear coloured maps
- Route photos and attractions on the way
- Updated directions

www.carreg-gwalch.com

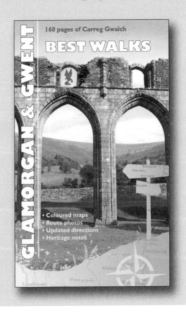

ANGLESEY

160 pages of Carreg Gwalch

BEST WALKS

• Coloured maps
• Route photos
• Updated directions
• Heritage notes

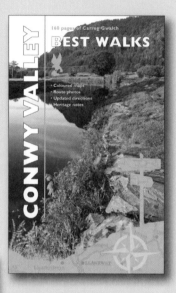

CONWY VALLEY

160 pages of Carreg Gwalch

BEST WALKS

• Coloured maps
• Route photos
• Updated directions
• Heritage notes

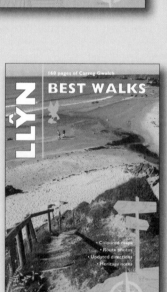

LLŶN

160 pages of Carreg Gwalch

BEST WALKS

• Coloured maps
• Route photos
• Updated directions
• Heritage notes

CLWYDIAN RANGE

160 pages of Carreg Gwalch

BEST WALKS

• Coloured maps
• Route photos
• Updated directions
• Heritage notes

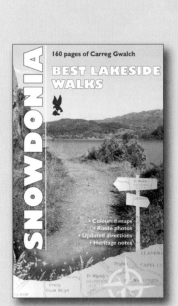

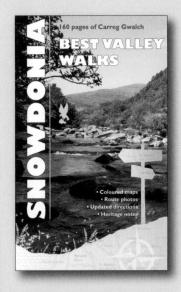

160 pages of Carreg Gwalch

BEST WALKS

CENTRAL WALES

- Coloured maps
- Route photos
- Updated directions
- Heritage notes

160 pages of Carreg Gwalch

BEST WALKS

BEACON MOUNTAINS

- Coloured maps
- Route photos
- Updated directions
- Heritage notes

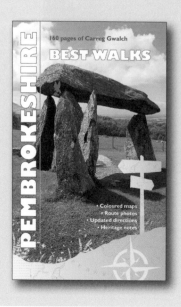

160 pages of Carreg Gwalch

BEST WALKS

PEMBROKESHIRE

- Coloured maps
- Route photos
- Updated directions
- Heritage notes

160 pages of Carreg Gwalch

GOWER

BEST WALKS
IN GOWER

Editor: Llywarch ap Myrddin

Pennard Burrows above Three Cliffs Bay